Mockingbirds at Jerusalem
A Poetic Memoir

By Rudolph Lewis

Mockingbirds at Jerusalem
A Poetic Memoir

By Rudolph Lewis

Rudolph Lewis - African-American Poetry
Revolutionary Consciousness - African Literature

All Rights Reserved Including the
right of reproduction in whole or in
part in any form

Copyright©2014 by Black Academy Press, Inc.
ISBN 0-87831- 041-X 978-0-87831-041-8 Paper

BLACK ACADEMY PRESS, INC.
4015 OLD COURT ROAD
PIKESVILLE, MARYLAND 21208 USA

Mockingbirds at Jerusalem: A Poetic Memoir

INTRODUCTION
By Rudolph Lewis

This poetic memoir recalls the place of my childhood, which was informed by a life of integrity and dignity, character qualities of maternal grandparents who taught me a respect for words, stories that shored up life diminished by ideas of separation and inferiority. It was a rural hamlet, named Jerusalem, founded in 1870, in Virginia's poorest county, Sussex. It offered grudgingly little in fields and forests, vision warped by slavery and Jim Crow.

This distorted place could and will never be one of permanence for a smart black boy. He will always seek to fulfill his self in other spaces. Jerusalem generates exiles. Beginning mid-1960s, I sought housing with indoor toilets and tap water, and joy in America's urban centers, and in a neo-colonial Congo, in New Orleans with poets, artists, musicians, educators, and priests. I worked as porter, teacher, journalist and librarian, studied modern art, listened to jazzmen, and passed out words against war and injustice during the American war against the Viet Cong.

When my exiled world became too cold and depressing to bear, I returned home to my grandmother's voice—her stories and songs. Most of these poems were first written in 2006 and have been in revision for seven years. They begin with a poem to my grandfather, William "Tinka" Lewis, who raised me as his son and died in 1970. There are many poems that call up my grandmother, Ella Lewis, whom I called "Mama" and from

Mockingbirds at Jerusalem: A Poetic Memoir

whom I learned our family history. In poor health she was suffering loss of weight and dementia.

Her daughter Annie made her comfortable in that home she and Tinka built in the late 1950s. The last family member of her generation, Mama had seen two of her daughters pass before her, and in the spring of 2008 both her son-in-law and then the daughter that bore me also passed. She was too ill to travel to Baltimore for either funeral. And in 2009 I became ill and she passed that December, a month after I married Yvonne Terry. I attempt to capture some of that disruptive beauty in these poems.

I owe an eternal debt to my maternal grandparents and their Jerusalem and all that made it live—our kinfolks, the dirt roads, the church community, Creath school, our neighbors, the gardens; barnyards and their pigs, mules, and chickens; the weather, dark purple nights with its stars. In this memoir I've tried to translate that beauty, horror, and wonder (and its end) into a contemporary idiom others may know.

I spent much of my time at the woodshed with Bobo Cat if not chopping wood, meditating, reading, and taking notes. I read the *Autobiography* of Amiri Baraka, Aldon Nielsen's *Black Chant*, and Nina Simone's *I Put a Spell on You*.

Some of the poems reflect those readings, like "Showdown at the Five Spot" and "I Put a Spell on We." The memoir recalls also Nathaniel Turner, the prophet of Southampton, who among others began the continuing tradition of the week-long August revival. Several poems sketch out the tragic death and funeral of Carter a multiracial child, the sadness of his mother and stepfather. "Ode for Walls," an ironical/symbolical poem, brings the memoir to a close.

Contents

Introduction by Rudolph Lewis 5

I
In My Father's House

My Father Still Comes to Me 13
Faraway But Not Dead Yet............................ 14
Jerusalem Nights 15
Bobo at Jerusalem 16
Chasing a Chastity Crown 17
Dionysius Unveiled 18
Tombstone for the Recent Dead 19
Lure of Yellow Jackets 20
Snakes Talking Tough 21
Steal a Penny off a Dead Man's Eye 22
Letting Jerusalem Do What It Does 23
My Mother Don't Like Country 24
Whippoorwill Sings at Midnight 25
A Rooster Crows before Sunrise 26
Mockingbird Sings Whippoorwill 27
Holy Days at Jerusalem 28
Shedding from the Inside 29
From the Outlands at Jerusalem 30
Aunt Oprah Incorporated 31

II

No Longer at Ease

Showdown at the Five Spot 33
Malcolm Is Dead! 34
No Soapboxes Here But Trees 35
Jerusalem in the Loop of the River 36
Dark Clouds Moving In 37
Mockingbird Sings in the Rain 38
Dark Clouds Hang Over Jerusalem 39
Sister Sadie Be What She Be 40
Wild Turkey Sacrificed at Jerusalem 41
Green Beans Harvested at Jerusalem 42
Mockingbird Chases a Crow 43
No Longer at Ease 44
Anthills at Jerusalem 45
Deep Down in the Sticks 46
New Orleans in My Soul 47
Tear's of the Devil's Wife 48
I Put a Spell on We 49
How I Long to be With You 50
Coming Through With the Spirit 51
Gardener in a State of Grace 52

III

Reaching Beyond My Self

Dancing Naked in a Maze 54
Which Doctor Knows Tomorrow? 55
Independence Day Weekend 56
Harlem Hot in My Mind 57
Living Above the Dismal 58
No Words for My Existence 59
In Need of Revolution   60
The Thrill Is Gone: A Blues Villanelle   61
Home Is Where Relief Is 62
Cousin Susie Moore Is Dead 63
Meditation on Insects 64
Get Up Dead Man: Blues Villanelle #2 65
Trinidad Lady at Club Paradise 66
Dreading Distrust & Reparations 67
Reparations Along the Nottoway 68
Reparations as Artful Enterprise 69
Divine Reparations Are Eternal 70
To Hell with Blackness & Nationalism 71

IV

August Revival

Resurrection 73
August Revival 74
My Woman Is This Forest 75
Romance Has No Natural Death.................................76
Women Who Care for the Weak 77
Chickens Coming Home..78
Loving That Other Man 79
Don't Say Goodbye to Truth 80
Good Night Sweet Irene 81
Last Call Dreaming 82
Dispelling the Darkness 83
Defying Raging Night 84
Up on Pisgah..85
Sonnet for 22 August 1831 86
Sonnet for Ancestors 87
Blind Woman with Guitar 88
Sonnet for Reality Men..89
War Is Not a Time of Joy 90
Sonnet for Albert Murray 91
Blues Sonnet for an Empty Bed 92
Women with Men in Prison 93
Mining Black Males 93
Under a Dark Cloud 95
Sonnet for Carter 96
Sonnet for Bailing Out..97
Ode for Walls 98

I

In My Father's House

My Father Still Comes to Me

When he died, I was not in the room, that bed where I slept as
a boy cold nights by a wood heater. Tinka built that room, that
house from ground, three cinderblocks high, eight rooms for
his family—that country of mules, outhouse, well dug with
pick & shovel. Mama pulled buckets, mud & clay heavy, for
water to drink, washed away fields & harvest. As he passed to
dreamland he took all that world. This house he left behind. A
sun goes down. I've come back to Tinka's home to conjure
that world, a backbreaker crosscut saw & ax splitting fire logs

& walking to school dirty miles & yellow bus faces screaming.
We waited by a highway, far too few words spoken. Trailways
Bus took me away to the city. I was sixteen. I began to be man
beyond the bounds of fields, barnyards, pigs & chickens. Books
& picket signs, college & blackness borne brave new worlds. In
flight I circle above. I'm not too unlike the father who raised me
silent & gloomy as he was in my years he wanted me to be him.
Mama his wife Ella & Ann his daughter nursed him through his
long illness after doctors cut his enlarged testicles—a disease no

one could pronounce. I visited home. He was in bed hiccupping,
prostrate, weak but for his earthmoving prayer to unseen powers.
Did he hear Him, that Negro God of so long ago who I learned to
fear in his voice, a heart he yearned silent? In dreams he comes to
me I forget he went away before I could know him. We strangers
learning in that house he kept building from the ground. Dreams
mirror that rough space. I was never homeless. Walls spin round.
He pulled me into his arms. We dancing whirling like dervishes.
Afraid of falling, I woke from my childhood when he went away.

Faraway But Not Dead Yet

Black night is crying. I hear drip-drops of water falling
from the eaves of my father's house. I'm in childhood
where a whippoorwill calls darkly deep in piney woods.
Train whistles blow at crossroads next to Jarratt Town.
Sounds chilled clear in Jerusalem air, soothing for ears,
barren of business street traffic. Last night I slept sound.
Chest & joint aching slid down a skull's warm clay well.
I look gently on an abandoned past: a golden mirror left
on living room wall by an off-and-on lover; three dusty

mirrors upstairs in the bathroom; a ragged box spring on
which I slept alone; a metal black table in large bedroom
where I wrote missives, & worked magic bones, a heavy
cabinet I pushed tight against the dining room window to
keep out homeless roaming men with shopping carts who
scout for boarded up houses with scrap metal they market
one more day. In the kitchen, there were dishes & glasses;
& more. Those items & those trucked away as garbage or
with me now fall short of memories I leave behind . . .

Jerusalem Nights

On a dark side new moon birds don't sing
midnight. On screen porch, a cool silence

early spring air, I wrap my legs in comfort.
Insects speak symphonic green forest pines.

Seamless, young deer from the woods steps
in stillness—delicate hooves in fresh garden.

He nibbles lips on tender sprouts. His meal
is no libation of lamb & lion lying down in

harmony. Hunger challenges art. I'm a poet
working purple sounds on a winding road.

A horn blows at crossroads, a heavy rumble.
Freight rushes south. I'm here home but not

all here. I sink deep in blood of rope & gun,
skin & cross. Ancestor ghosts haunt my life.

Bobo at Jerusalem

1st Monday home. Sun is still below forest horizon.
Blue sky matted with white gold-tinged clouds, it's

me & Bobo at the mouth of the woodshed. We cool:
a jacket & cap, no air stirs treetops filled with songs.

Silencing forest sounds: a dove's coos in rising sun
glow; a goose upholsters his lone flight with honks.

Smelling a free, easy meal a stray dog peeps around
the shed, spies me, breaks away. I'm in a cat defense

with a stick in hand/harsh words, a mock run across
a sprouting garden. Brown dog gets lesson. In fright

Bobo endured long dark night alone in outhouse. My
buddy stretches out & naps. I fear my folk tradition:

they don't like cats in house. Dangers thunder as we
meditate an end. I empty out a life of wail like slop.

Chasing a Chastity Crown

My eyes this last night of April are a purple carpet
of stars. The moon reclines on its back holding up

the rains, crosses a grassy field & sinks into silent
pines. Ten days ago I crossed the Nottoway, again,

its trembling black waters, a river known to slave-
holding Jerusalem. A man is dead & buried, bullet

behind the ear. No holy war news. But gang trials,
cleaning dirty laundry. Our filth's flashing outline,

gun-blazing bitterness. Greed & lust are alphabets
we learn on streets, every hamlet. Rocks & money,

glass pipe smoke clouding the pulse beat of a blues.
With nimble-wings we plot to kill our dying fathers.

Dionysus Unveiled

In his younger days floating down stream the drawbridge
had to be raised when he puffed ganja weed, blew smoke
rings with Rastas and New Orleans artists. Sisyphus & his

burden was a myth like Marie Laveau and her fountain of
youth, bundled mojo tales of graveyard dirt & flying over
walls. He conjured lovers with pretty, like a Big Chief of

Mardi Gras, tragedian adrift in watercolor minds. He woke
in morning fog, his sweet executioner banging on his door,
blowing horns, black-gowned from a night out on the town.

He raised some cash & escaped north in his orange VW in
the dark of night. He was a raging god then with a mighty
arm, never a father but a wooly scapegoat on Suicide Rock.

Tombstone for the Recent Dead

In this waking season of freshly turned soil, disked and raked,
a garden of greens rise moist hand-high. Four men waved this

world above goodbye: Lanky Lee, would-be millionaire; Stout
Sticky, card player; Young Nelson, chemical worker; Switch-

Blade Cigar, the finisher. All black & dead: on a vacation from
which they will never return. For them no weekends, Saturday

nights of Rum & Coke—bid whist & shit-talking after a Boston.
Policies on the living postponed, in flux. On River Styx there'll

be no cash-in on the dead—no wills pass on to those who enjoy
the cool of spring mornings, no downing the eight ball in corner

left from the green rail, no witch flights from tokes on a coke
pipe. When the hearse pulls into the cemetery all's left behind.

Lure of Yellow Jackets

I tell my own story: Alas, age not madness overtakes me.
The counselors of confusion who seek no good end, their
words tread upon my heels. They placed bets: my tongue
would wither thin in this forest clime, my rural rumblings
would move only crumbs for ants to cart away; I'd be lost
like a ghost in green woods after busy Druid Hill Avenue,
grasping roots would break like china on a con man's jaw.
I can stand up against OK-corral parasite politics. I broker

no fear of gangster hit men on frontier corners. I metaphor
carpenter bees boring in 2 x 4s, sighing pines, sunshine on
tombstones. I'll lash poison-poured-in-ear plotters to rock
beds with stout rope. Fire burns sponges in my revenge pit.
Blue birds utter silences that water the spirit. My brain will
not stoop, like a fool hugging the hating love of intolerance.
Jimi's guitar sounds shatter skulls of big bellies with weak
knees. I pare my growls only by half—my pen dangles free.

Snakes Talking Tough

Cold. Damp. No stars shine thru dark clouds like my sweet lover's eyes. Her magnolia-brown arms seize me & ring me into stratospheric delights of bee-bop curves. Her yum-yum boned might raise the dead if hoisted & tongued as Satchmo his coronet. Some kings can. I'm a blue crossroad. Midnight fires burn my wooly skull. It's two weeks since she ran away with a matrix of punters, adorned cacklers, grass & air heads bucking, warring over turf. Sirens blare & blue lights flash as jackals bellow like a volcano. In her dreams I'm barbed wire

in dark alleys off Pennsylvania Avenue. She has a man who plays stride piano with Satan's hands. Her phone boast is tea leaves soaking in the steam room of my ancestors. Sun burns away the fog of our spring-day separation. I diet on onions & garlic to ward away any canine teeth in my heart's veins. I've stretched out under shimmering-shadow mysteries of trees as mocking bird naps. I breathe nature's piney breath, her aroma soothes, her weather dowses my mind's brushfire. Austere in my habits, my last tears dry hard like a rock. I'm a steady roll.

Steal a Penny off a Dead Man's Eye

—for Grover Reid

Don't let them speak longer than half hour over my body
if it remains whole at my death. Make it brief like a poem

of a great poet: no lying snapshots of my life. If what I am
fell short of wealth and boons, let my pauper life be. Turn

your back, walk away. I need—stretched out for eternity in
my grail—neither poses nor asides from family and friends.

All not done, before my cushioned coffin, let my blackness
reign. No eulogy—people singing, walking golden shoes in

a cloudy beyond; no false testimony about no complaints—
fill a wagon drawn by a mule team with hooch. If song you

need, "I'm Soldier on the Battlefield." Tip a bottle of aged
white moonshine to hardships of mothers. In memory, I'd

drink hardy & chew soulful. Close the lid, toss the dirt, pray
for freedoms yet to come, & let writing/fighting be forever.

Letting Jerusalem Do What It Does

Sunday morning pastiche: red oak by the driveway
of blue rocks. Its girth bulges middle age. A breeze
stirs green leaves. A boy hung a sand bag from one
of its limbs. Angry fists crushed ribs of known foes,
revelers of ruin & mourning. I inherited dark clouds
green western horizons. Suns refused to rise beyond
a pine & a cedar grown immense since my younger
weedy years. An old black gum shaded a barn filled
with corn & pea vines, flanked by two mule stalls—

all gone. The forest sings a friend's silence: sparrow
tweets; a red-breasted robin whistles; a somber dove
blows his notes. My aged bones romance childhood
learned between covers of other lives. I forget a year
the sun sank as mockingbird chatters. The dredge silt
of urban shadows come: women ply corner arts, men
swallow thunder wine; blood-curdling sirens blow life
down to rusty knees I left behind. Sit with me awhile
& listen, dear sods, I'm at mouth of the woodshed
with a book, my scribble pad sketches out a ghostly
mule of youth. It brays uneasy in Daddy's barnyard.

My Mother Don't Like Country

She's gone now. I was standing on the roof when she waved
again to return to her life in the city. Brief reunions fall short
crossing family histories of whys & choices we never wanted.
Abandonment, grudges, hurt feelings fester on & on when we
end to begin from the beginning. Truths are on a lift going up
& down never found as they were. This memory only I know:
A full moon purple night, she escaped a Creath farm by Sansi

Swamp—Depression sharecropping, at seventeen with child in
her belly, for electric streetcars. No shotgun greetings in dark
spaces or stars in ghetto/slums, no skeleton closets. She chose to
leave me in her father's world to maid & seamstress & birth
five more. Her child became Mama's baby, a man who waves
farewell from a roof her father left behind. As sister & brother,
we grew apart, unable to re-cross that bridge. Big Dipper fades

in flashing neon. She with aching back created a new life, left
hoeing fields for hotel & factory, for tap water & indoor toilets.
She's retired, spying spellbound exiles from her window. Like
grandmas, she frees hands & minds of her daughters. Thunder
booms. Spring lightning cracks. On a limb, Mockingbird sings.
Pear leaves shimmer sharp edged shadows. Eyes open to whys,
I survey blue sky roof, forest horizon, & mothers who give life.

Whippoorwill Sings at Midnight

I'm in eastern woods this damp chilly night. Above
a church cemetery, a yellow moon peeps thru pines.

I'm a lonesome train blowing whistles at crossroads.
New Orleans salty fog streets wash up in my mind's

debris floating; the dazed paddling, wading in water
welling tears above brown cheeks—displaced, raped.

Shotgun houses squat like big-eyed children starving.
Hands wave from rooftops; we on living-room sofas.

Danziger bridge cover-up murder, media cameras cap
lens against our blackness. Uptowners suck oysters in

shells, drink coffee, chew beignets, poets & musicians
banished. Dixieland plays on Bourbon behind ancient

bricks. Strut/dance. 2nd liners color dark-ceiling cries
for the gone—black flood waters rising raise the dead.

A Rooster Crows before Sunrise

Thinking death is cold morning-air shifting south
like white corkscrews. Life can be tragic at noon.
Limbs wave. Pines rock back and forth like black
women to gusts of sadness—on a sunny day. Blue
smoke wafts out from under a black pot of greens.
A lone sparrow tweets, a tiller airs soil for garden
plants. A jagged blade lacerates grass in road ditch
near Jerusalem church. My mother's lover crossed

a dead/dream border to remind me of life with him.
In cemetery with brothers, a sister, his mother, she
lowered down late 80s, was laid, under marble top
near Deacon Joe Dick/1956, year of muddy rumor.
I turned 8. We make peace with our past, knowing
we can never go back. "Mack the Knife" populates
pathways in all. We go far & no farther. Bluesmen
huckabuck time above dusty floors of rock and roll.

Mockingbird Sings Whippoorwill

—for Amiril Baraka

Today, my mind is a knotty sheep's ass. Truths
shade/shift tree leaves—the pages of my book.
Poets have no fantail at Jerusalem. Animals rule:
they slither, crawl, walk on or below earth, or fly.

Clouds, stars & moon are small sky streams, flow
down into consciousness. I'm meandering muddy
Nottoway. What's my story? A bee capers flower
to flower. Sparrows play love on red oak limb. A
cool breeze dances a black butterfly. I am no hero

like a squawking crow. He passes over on his way
to green fields. A brilliant red cardinal on the lawn I
toss a kiss for christening. He lights in a corn bin.
My soul's eyeless. Bobo crashes dry leaves & pine
straw. Snakes slide among trees in silence. The cat

herds a horse-whipper for the kill. The shiny beast
escapes teeth & claws, comes under my pen. I know
a crawling toast, a crab kind of pride. Stub-necked, I
end it: I cracked his dome & tossed him in woods.

Holy Days at Jerusalem

White exhaust—an east bound jet streaks blue
sky like a bright scar on a woman's belly. It's

another Sunday morning, quiet, a cool breeze a
hot sun. Cabbage plants aired grow like boys

to men. Black pot, mouth to the ground, drown
escape plans for the sons of Nathaniel's ancient

Holy Ghost, blue-black draught of forgetfulness
by owners of shiny cars & brick houses. Canaan

Land is any place where blues is not. Black sins
eye blessings from blond Jesus. I water tomato

plants, fan away bumble bees & wasps. All days
are holy if work is more than a paycheck. Dark

clouds roll in as the sun goes down. A pole light
gathers flying insects. Bats swoop in for dinner.

Shedding from the Inside

I am that white-breasted mockingbird perched on
a branch of a dead pine, my back to blue evening,

singing backwater tunes my ancestors sang for me,
spirit of forget & forgive. My own way, I bow, fly

to the lawn & feed on insects, as birds do. Sparrow
tweets memories of red oak. My songs are branches

on which he clings. In purple shadows, blues soars,
above suffering like a prophet walking on a stormy

sea. A dark riddle is mere upholstery for crossbones.
Mockingbird speaks more tragic than skulls on posts.

From the Outlands of Jerusalem

Woodshed etched out in evening shadows. I'm
dark clouds on courthouse lawn: Walter Cotton
lynched ten miles from where I played as a boy
in woods of Jerusalem. A Confederate military
statue stands with rumbling thunder. I retreat in

fog smoke as Lee's gray army before blue coats.
Tyranny then as ubiquitous as blacks in clanking
chains searching for self, granite values heavy as
an anvil, meaningful as freedom, lasting as magic
streets of the imagination. His mama was a slave
after Jubilee, handed him to a white man to break

a spirited animal behind eyes where art is created.
Life is more than a Monticello con job, more than
the whips of manliness. I was a boy of 9 growing
silent in rage & shame of black field hands when
Little Rock hate was New World for kids like me.
Mingus sang "Fables of Faubus." Martin wringed

a dream from evil. JB got up slowly off his knees,
then cracked helmet skulls. Jimmy had scribbled
notes on Dick Wright's blues as Trujillo damned
blackness. Capote beat the devil on white screens.
Tim Posten cried, "LeRoi, What you eating now?"

Aunt Oprah Incorporated

I'm running again in a wooded nightmare, bloodhounds
chasing a scent of their master's bedchamber. I'm a last
go round, losing a hunch. High John the Conqueror finds
no black enigmas in official case studies? No Texas T in
our backyards. What's up: Bruh Rabbit wears black tails
for Bugs? He's ballroom dancer at Smalls café. Michael
bounces Memphis Minnie, a Mississippi queen, twisting
her life away in a hoop, as Joe the Slugger wins his bout.

Who loves our blindfolded children more than eyehole tv?
Whose daughters, Mr. Monticello Jeff? Whose sons wade
in floods of garbage, floating bodies filled with cornflakes?
Wolves boogie on black beauties. Dream what comfort we
can be to poor mothers. Sunshine trees: no guilty verdicts.
Shadows recede. Mockingbird beats his drum, singing on a
tall pine as flock of buzzards circle over white mansions.

II

No Longer at Ease

Showdown at The Five Spot

Gun slinging Duels resurrect time: earth/space, Ra's bamboo boat. We LeRoi & Ishmael master brothers destined as bull dog fighters like Osiris & Set are in mad love with Isis, who's on kinky knees shooting craps, dice tossed against brick walls. Stagolee & Billy too are eternal. A wife prays; we speak in her ear. Our struggles thrill a mind like cocaine, brushfire burning. Cemetery smoke wafts, hangs. Words speak/mirror stones

& silence. Sexual magic birthed a Freud & Jung to father cigar envy in neighbor's ass. Bird plays the coming of Trane; dawn windows fresh being. Hips loom a new rhythm god. Piano jukes Horus howling at Sansi Swamp. Hot mama burns down master's plantation to ash. None wants to see her hurt in a 21st century blues. Sunrise shines in tall black gum tree. I divine a god-self on yellow pad.

Mockingbirds at Jerusalem: A Poetic Memoir

Malcolm Is Dead!

Early a Memorial Day morning, Death is not
my mind, not even honoring the dead. White

fog hangs over a cornfield heavy from the sky
to a swamp loam below. Tomato and cabbage

plants rise almost a foot above their bed. Birds
are alive with a murmuring chatter. It's spring.

Around my shoulders I drape an Indian blanket
woolly warm. I sit by the woodshed. I searched

all night: periods & commas of LeRoi's friends:
Olsen, Dorn & Creely. Read how Roi slipped in

Black Mountain. He jazzed up shows in Harlem
with his pen, his .45 under his belt. His art was

beat down so many times. A wordsmith whose
warriors stumble & fall. Each man has his day

in Mockingbird's field; harvest grain's left to
mice. Dew falls. Our backs lean to rising sun.

No Soapboxes Here But Trees

I'm a last quarter moon, reclining like an old man in
rocking chair, dreaming what was and what might
have been. We follow the route of all things. Seeds

drop, sprout, & show leaf like my garlic bulb there on
the table. We gather & store as all rodents do. Forest
people pray we may grow in a greater plowed earth.

We look to the sky & no rain comes in forecast. Dirt
dauber waits caught in black spider web. Life goes on

without. Robin & sparrow sing freely while woodpecker
rat-a-tat-tats on dead pine by dying church. The wind
rushes across those stretched out in cemetery. Train roars

across pine treetops. Life's sketched out for us if we
dawdle like color & line on canvas take their shapes.
Mockingbird squeals what must be said in mischief.

Jerusalem in the Loop of the River

Freedmen came on us wandering, 1870 when cool
breezes rustle green leaves of an oak & sweet gum.
We the banned needed a place to call home, nearby

pines & cedar where mockingbird has a storehouse
for his ever-changing tunes, toss a kiss on wings to
cardinal play in the cemetery hickory. Color walls

& people geography changing at Jerusalem. Faiths
not ours build luxury retreats for up-north kinsmen.
We refuge now for strangers to slough off whiffing

a line of cocaine. Strangers move in Miss Geneva's
trailer after passing. A yellow-jacket flight yellows
brain paths, dying with a twist of the wrist. You/me

& clouds fade like one-night love affairs. Me/night
walk out the heat of the sun. Bobo cat whines, steps
like a soft-footed, seesaw sweetie, a loft of laughter.

Dark Clouds Moving In

A poem can't cool out the disquiet inside me,
as I cakewalk untaught channels to childhood.
I slide clouds over house & fields as sweating
lovers. Thunder rumbling voices, cool chilling
air & fifth-decade anxieties. Oak limbs thrash.

Pines gust purple-bark women who ride bare
back history's prospects of lightning strikes,
how it cracks skies & hearts. Charm me, babe,
Sweet Kokomo. Like my gardener who plows
we drop rose seeds for birds & growing plants.

We may fall one line short in a rickety carriage
of poetry. Bird boned, hip-hop rhymes grow up
in ashes we breast fed. For words will & testify
a fresh midday downpour when poets compose
as if every day is Friday. Scales fall from eyes.

Mockingbird Sings in the Rain

At early dawn in a hickory tree I'm a cemetery voice that wants his family back the way they were before I left at sixteen. Water-laden clouds slide down dark from western mountains. The forest awakes in sound: a cricket, then crows over by the church scream caw for caw. Life as was slips deeper in dark corridors of my brain aging toward sixty summers that will never come back fully. Mama was in the kitchen cooking a country breakfast to welcome me back where I was a boy who could plow a mule, pick cotton, shake peas.

My dreams drip drop from eaves & land into puddles. Here's Bob White he too is a traveler moaning. I blow my fists in answer. Miles down winding roads a train whistles, rumbling cars head north with heavy load. A dog barks in the southern woods. Remnant is all that I retain. On the screen front porch flies buzz satisfaction. A neighbor's rooster awakens/crows rally beyond trees. We begin one more day on a buzzard's wing of hope & despair. He was a fool for years, they say, dark suits on way to burying ground. The end leaves all hurts behind.

Dark Clouds Hang Over Jerusalem

The family that lives loves together is a fiction
of long forest nights. High star-filled dark skies
spare me gunfire & drug streets—I getting used.
There're always rats entering homes, and biting
a child. A knifing fine rain begins to slice faces
after half moon set in woods behind open fields.
I am no turning clockwise brain. I'll be mad to
camouflage forest green pines a pastoral across
the road from a cemetery. At the gate I forget I

was a 9 to 5er. My ear grounding sounds in dark
hours like a black cast iron pot. A slave screen for
plot & deception. The smoke shields us from
stinging mosquito mouths. Legs warmed, water
drops steadily on the tin roof. There red oak leaf
slides/downs bodies of water below. Lawns rise
up. I'm heavy sky morning, falling in flute notes,
drowsing like silk. I lay in empty room, a bridge
to cross mud ponds. Mockingbird wakes the sun.

Sister Sadie Be What She Be

Bone-ache in cool moist air. Mockingbird is silent. A half-moon night in western purple sky chilled by last night's storm. Over in darkness, whippoorwill speaks his name as if we can forget long ago when beyond rain soaked fields of blue green forests our walnut ancestors tread with brute-backs in bloody-whip regimes in their struggle for freedom & faith,

in crude under garments fashioned-tossed meal bags, letters boiled away in pig grease lye. In gingham & wool, cotton stockings & laced brogans they slaved not too far removed from all that crawled, walked or flew above swamps, as patriarchs stood foot in door. Silence burrows through beak, mouth & purse, rolls in blankets before race/sex altars as the moon curves.

Wild Turkey Sacrificed at Jerusalem

Our grandmas, like their freed grandmas, survived on
diet of coons, possums, squirrels & wild turkeys. They
skinned & pulled feathers; oven-hot & pit-fire embers,
meat seasoned with potatoes & spices to make game fit
for tables. But we had to ask Mama how we de-feather a
dead turkey in the bed of her son-in-law's truck, road-
killed in a fit of madness. I'd driven roads with animals
crossing over. I've never come close to striking a wild
turkey. Beauty emblems like freedom deman respect.
Still I'm not blameless: night wandering to Jerusalem, I

tire tracked a family of coons. That bright turkey day by
woodshed I wanted to feel the bush, bloodlust felt by my
ancestors—that urgency of hunger. My hands were mine
yet theirs pulling dry feathers from white flesh. Split him
open, I fingered/scooped maw & grass. Readying him for
a woman's touch. Ann lowered him in water pot brought
to boil. His flesh stank rank swamp water. No morsel for
Old-Time's sake reached any mouth. Dish for dogs on no
kill list. We shoo ghosts back to tall grasses of Nadowa's
forest, like we Chano, conga god, gunned down in brawl.

Green Beans Harvested at Jerusalem

When I think back, my life seems like sleepwalk, but
not an in-ness smell of the soul's apple orchard. I look
way out. I return to boyhood as a moth to bright flame,
as scholar visiting a molding archive. I jot down notes
of misery & mystery on yellow-lined paper. I turn into
a distant voice: western-woods whippoorwills, wailing
jazz coronet full moon. I hang black clouds a sky float
toward the ocean. I pine forest horizon, space deserted

by freedmen, who cleared away trees & roots, dug wells
& outhouses, raised houses, barns & woodsheds when I
was a budding thought. Sun & moon revolve around me.
Fiery earth filled green beans with warmth. I was a hand
caressing leaves by my window. Morning dew & foggy
night savor coffee cups. In sandals & bib overalls, I pick
beans after bunches, no urgency. On kitchen table, work.
Ann, Mama, & I snap ends, break halves, toss/pile them

to be blanched/stored in freezer bags. Tumbler time fades
skin white in photo album. We laugh, dance, coin words in
tedium. A half-boiled turkey speaks to dogs. Absent is
Miss Lula Bell, at 94, as she courts gossip, drives church
to church. I may never embrace again soft dreams I hold of
green pines piercing sky blue notes & memory. Dying in
them I escape the dead in the church cemetery. I wager it
all: page-crumbling dangers, yearning loving never was.

Mockingbird Chases a Crow

I walked awhile in shoes of Negro farmers behind a mule,
Jim Crow days of plow handles & lines held steady to turn

budding earth. In a blue sky under thin white clouds a half
moon follows setting suns, falling below pine tops. I played

in nature's drama of harvest & renewal. Today, over a hill,
I, a gardener, split ground with motorized tillers. From tree

to tree and across the lawn with songs, robins and sparrows
frolic & feast. No salt or sting in any mood. Worship camps

out. Lettered preachers on the move know Parable of Seeds
when swamps are rich & mockingbird gives chase to crow.

No Longer at Ease

I walk the floor hours an addict in withdrawal. New moon is a silent dark night of grasshoppers, crickets, & frogs at my window. My brain is a prison of birds.

A dove moans, whippoorwill speaks to cloudless stars that spin around the heavens. From my oriental carpet watermelon & black walnut seeds take root & spread.

Corn stalks grow high as a ceiling. In this green bean darkness of southern discord mockingbird is on a red oak limb in the leaves singing a blues of spring's end.

Anthills at Jerusalem

I search forest green for a 12-year-old who dreamt
farm life on purple evenings when thunder booms.

Sun rays rise, peep through pine & black gum trees
in chilly silence. That life broke off like bark when

mockingbird sang his gray goodbye. Morning goes
on always: rooster crows whippoorwill. My skull's

birdcage is masked red & black for cardinal at corn
bin, a subtle theft of storehouse meals. Circumspect

on buzzard wings I soar above combat fields. Death
is a busy man. On green front lawn, a hundred hills

by worker ants. Building nest in standing dead pine
hard head woodpecker drums good things like blues.

My memory dances with ghostly lost friends inside
garden-ripen tomatoes, uncrowns crabgrass at roots.

Deep Down in the Sticks

We relive in dying. Ole Tinka of Jerusalem never
turned his back on warm summer days & blue sky
after rains, foot-deep in drying mule-plowed fields.

He tied stabs to tomato plants for its red fruit. He's
green breeze rustling oak-tree leaves, thunder fists
deep in an eastern wood. I tore away from seasons

of plant & harvest & ran as a Greyhound/Trailways
rolled north on 301. My life stinks of street corners
& beat-downs North & McCullough, midnite-alley

gunshots. Coke pipes sucking up rooms & women
nowhere to go. I've come back: hands/toes in ashes
of my ancestors. I wash tub spring kale for smoked

pig jowls in an old cast iron pot on wood fire. Black
butterfly flutters flower bush & disintegrates darkly.
I nod into a forest landscape. My cat's stretched out

by my chair, waits to prowl sunset in sparrow/mice.
We'll ever be a mouth shade of a ragged woodshed:
me & a dream friend click & sip ice-cold lemonade.

New Orleans in My Soul

For four years I was Louisiana, behind the sun—
Monroe, Baton Rouge, & New Orleans, nativity
of salty women/magic in their step, running wild
music in bayou veins. Canal Street, a bridge way
between a whorl of poets. The arms of Jerusalem

drew me home. Swampy summers a sanctuary for
minds & senses when cool breezes lap skin. Bees
bumble buzz lawns for mockingbird silence. Slow
sun sinks below the jagged green horizon. Combat,
beer & hard-time winds strike palpable abuse into

deep crevices of callous hands. Thunder booms me.
My life races in tunnels; war time drags on. I can't
shut out the now/past: grassland school days, hail
above pine tops, or a boy lying in strawberry fields.
Now is everywhere as Satchmo blows crystal roses.

Tears of the Devil's Wife

My grandma was a woman who endured like her
grandma who disquieted her freedom generation.
They stepped soundless like a cooling steady rain.
Here in these lynched-heated southern woods, we
ever under dark hanging clouds & usurping winds.

My grandma's timed flashes were never language
easily gotten around. She groaned barbwire desire.
When an 8-year-old boy, I cried, yanked her aged
skirt. She pried shotgun from hands of a god-riled

grandfather full of thunder & lightning's dangerous
speech. In a forest beyond cemeteries she charmed
the faithless in oracular hieroglyphs stretching out
unlocking heaven's vault. In spite inherited cracks
she made us emblematic of wholeness. Rhinoceros

tears brown mountain cheeks of history. Unbeaten
in her rapture we wash away the red-eyed dreams.
Our lives reboot, waking with God's booming jabs.

I Put a Spell on We

—for Nina Simone

We've scars others refuse to see from places we've
traveled from oak to pine like any other people. We
drag alone burdens, a racial task. Tinka grows old on
front-porch. The sun casts shifting shadows. Clouds
move in from south like Death. Mama waits for him

slave child & sharecroppers. Their final rest expands
under hickory in lawns soaked in mockingbird blood.
I gather ancient spiritual energy. Eye cataracts bluing
to keep her belief going in re-skinned rhythms yet to
come. Their minds dip into clay wells unsung where

generations are built on borders. Buckets of shouting
drawn, praises poured out to grow gardens. Sparrows
tweet-tweet on a line of church saints & backbiters. I
awake on Sunday morning cat eyes on a green carpet.
Hoeing fields, we pull wire grass from beans & peas.

How I Long To Be With You

In the South, sun, wind, rain dominate like confederate statues dwarfing us on courthouse lawns. Restless even in death, their lives are not ours. Downpour screened on

front porch. Frogs croak/water falls. Mosquitoes, size of humming birds, whine. Cat under arm I'm moving inside. Mockingbird sings. Resistive we pray for rescue when no

omen but dove moans. River rises in discords. An artist's life is a soothsayer palm, flowing lines for a spider's web. Raindrops dance for an echoing spirit. My window pane's lithe & clean, sharp as an edge. Fantasizing skulls sashay damsels in bloody silks thrusting deep an assassin's sting.

Coming Through with the Spirit

I'm at that sunlight special time when rainfall
streaks. Clouds blush bluish-orange in a moist

calm twilight. The arms of Aunt Sarah lengthen
reaching up to the heavens as she gathers spirits

to her bosom. Bob White whistles. Breezes lick
tree leaves like prancing fingers on piano keys.

In masks we vanquish days of storm, we steer in
joy-drum parade. I fold clothes in red basket. We

blanket night stretching darkly. A crescent moon
sinks in dark horizon. Crickets cry mercy, mercy.

Gardener in a State of Grace

Nina's jazz is a way of thinking African. In her
garden she's the yes-life of falling pollen tassels
upon corn silk—there will be kernels lined up in

a row, sacrificing ears to pull/shuck. She parents
how to say Hell No to way we make profit, leads
to where we are. Running limas reach upon wires

to sky. She holds up humanity's body weight &
digs deeper than rigs of Texas-T for illumination.
Tomatoes grow waist high budding green size of

golf balls. Her bounteous spirit overarches times
of fiery declension. Lady bugs have feasted. She
drops to knees & bears her breasts before earth's

marble rogue gods & execs succoring global tits.
Hour-glass trading-mobs garrison the world. We
breach walls to music poppy gardens called Nina.

III

Reaching Beyond the Self

Dancing Naked in a Maze

Seven o' clock in the morning, Mama, 94, kitchen table—milk, Eggo—her motored wheelchair, says "I want you to turn my mattress." Her night terrors

make out an haunting dreamscape: her room under the bed a nameless black man shines light. Stunned by her kingdom of apparitions, I did not stir the air,

damp & heavy. Her dark-eyed revelation liked that of a hashish smoker: angels walking water, a choir singing up in heaven when crickets are flexing their

legs in a dark forest, or night creatures crawling as fear in the fevered minds of city folk. The sun was rising. Bats had made their exit. Mockingbird came

on stage singing. My world limp green lettuce says, "Mama, it was nothing," to calm brain cells, falling ashes of hard-time dreams: ghosts visit as they will.

Which Doctor Knows Tomorrow?

Aging has no cure but death. 94, Mama is under covers with backache. I am wary of doctors of trapdoor stripe, artists of life & dying, no promises one way or another.

I'm reading *Freedom in the Dismal*, a novel. An on-tv breaks silence. We're twice a child, old folks say. Side to side, she rolls. Early evening she ate Bojangles fried

chicken heartily. We have pillar moments on the down slope. An owl hoots in the western wood below waxing moon. Buzzards roost in pines beyond an apple orchard

too close to the house. Sue Gal, Mama's daughter across the way on hill, feeds them her leftovers of deer carcass, a white gift. I uproot their nesting banging a sheet of tin.

I wander from porch to woodshed, reifying Jim Jordan & his spinning globe, Nina Simone's Atlantic doctor rolling bones of cryptic signs. On the Dumas plantation, a Negro dismally adds, "The only freedom man gets in this world is how he will die." I have no hoary quarrels that come to nothing. In restless dreams, Mama wakes to a rising sun.

Independence Day Weekend

Dew is heavy on the grass as the sun with
golden rays mounts the black gum tree by
the garden's edge. Under a blue sky I'm
wrapped in a Mexican wool blanket. Crows
rally. Mockingbird, Sparrow, and Robin fly
tree to tree in song as Rooster wakes. In his
black mask Cardinal whistles wind on an
electric line, swoops into the corn bin.
Bobo, cat food on his breath, yet he still
prowls the lawn. In her wheelchair, Mama
is ready for breakfast. This is a good
Sunday to testify in Jerusalem's woodshed
mouth. Love promises red fruit for all blues
songs. Sunrise glows orange in pine trees.

Harlem Hot in My Mind

Breezes stir in green leaves but it's still a hundred, hot as
red potbelly stove stoked with coal in a Negro church in an
August revival, saints running up & down the aisle
testifying the Lord's sweet goodness. Sweat soaked. I'm in
shade—hot as if the super in the summer has turned up heat
20 degrees with no prior notification to force tenants to
vacate bequeathed space. . . That's been an underlying
dread, the degradation for a day and ever—how to stand up
in the pressure cooker of aging existence, how to be manly
beyond our fears & theirs—to be or not to be slaves in hell.
Mockingbird dismisses worries & so crows mind their p's &
q's when they fly/step in their hood—got wings & beaks to
keep 'em at bay and there ain't no sheriff, gun, or tanks

cruising streets like in Baghdad, no gunships like in Gaza
that's gonna even odds. Rouge lips be black ops in feasting-
table illusions—regime change smell like pig to those who
dream America in the slums of Islamabad—who hasn't lost a
mother like Jerusalem, we've called refuge & home? Who
speaks of what we got when they want—they swat down
doors to splinters, guns drawn, we face down on the floor in
fear of the law; bulldoze houses for overpasses, for spite or
blight; drop a bomb, kill women & children; for love & care
to make life jack boot-hard, so taxes can't be paid. There's a
rich pundit ready to justify or testify, or scheme with opium
or moonshine or smallpox blanket or Bigger Thomas—some
story of fathers as insects for those who want to win it all.

Living above the Dismal

Mockingbird augurs morning pains, my mood indigo.
He flies from hickory in the cemetery to the porch, to
woodshed to cheer me to a life above the tidal—like
devoted lovers come back home. The scales of critics
shift, slide a balance for poets trapped in war, demise,

heartless murder, shameless starvation. I'm a Jim Boy in
a self-exile scribbling to make sense of absurdities, a
roll of dice, behind bars, in libraries turning pages of
academic progress of people caught between granite &
cold steel. Hope fades; sand runs out the hour glass for
freedom. They got us in life. There's no way I'll adjust
to a waltz, laying my head on virgin laps, tasting melon
wetness on sweet lips. I mark days with toenails. Insect
darkness. I won't shrink from threats. Black hands held

loft my childhood. Waiting thirty years may not be long
for a new world, but a breathless bore. I'll dream beyond
the flesh of my father's house—springs & blue sky, cool
nights, buttercups & bluebells, green lemon tea, wooded
paths. I listen to mockingbird—full moon pines horizons.

No Words for My Existence

Life's blackness ever changes here in the ponds, swamps, streams of the Nottoway in this great expanse of forests above the Dismal Swamp. All this moisture feeds the sky shades of blue, orange & gray before & after storms. If English had richer syntax we'd have hundreds of names of rains just for the summer months that fall in this village, we call Jerusalem. Words multisyllabic, long as limbs of tall knotty pines. Words possessed with slave peculiarities, like the movement of the sun & moon; shape & color of clouds; out of what forest it comes into a civilized clearing. Its duration—longer than a shower shorter than a hurricane. Is mockingbird singing or quiet? What's growing, garden & field; what harvest now a fruit?

Who died & what was plowed under? Does it creep & crawl like a snake, as it approaches or burst upon us like a mad dog; or rush across tree tops like a train, or does it crash down like foot bucket emptied on a head or in moving driving sheets, from all directions all at once, with thunder & lightning (its volume & flashes—how it shifts from woods to woods)? Which way trees rock, limbs sway & thrash about? How raindrops hit roof or side of the house? How it runs off eaves to puddles below. And when it goes, is the air cool like cedar green or hot & steamy like purple roses or foggy like milk film on a glass? It'd take red natives of these environs or an African in these green forests to coin regional words. Or a poet at a court of leisure a lifetime to note the comings & goings of the hand of God.

In Need of Revolution

Trees & persons are harvested at Jerusalem (Jarratt & Sussex) as much if not more than was done back in slavery time when Ol' TJ was at Monticello. Evening skies no threatening clouds that drift in from the north. Sun sets a red globe over its wood process plant & state penitentiary. Twilight orange halo glow above pines. Full moon shines in a purple southern sky tonight.

I am chilled in this cool summer air. Days ago a storm lay open a structure in need of repair. Mockingbird evades the horrors of our lives. I have been climbing ladders, lately. I found source of the leaks in the woodshed that stores prayers and poetic feelings. I ripped off the tar roofing—worked up a backbreaking sweat & found a hole in a board the size of a fist. Filled with black rot &

moisture, the boards buckled. Neglect and shoddy work always bring such crises when all suffer below. For a building to last & serve well, patching is no answer: the whole needs to be ripped, every plank and rebuilt with new wood under the curve of a new moon: a carpenter's erection that'll be able to weather the years.

The Thrill Is Gone: A Blues Villanelle

I'm in flight under a spell; I wish you well.
Can't you feel me, falling, my back breaks?
Yes, rock me; roll me like a wagon wheel.

You strawberries on top a lighthouse cone.
You Double Dutch, my ice cream & cake
I'm from under your spell; I wish you well.

Roll me, Baby, pull covers down my dome.
Do me sweetie, do me for old time's sake.
Yes, rock me; roll me like a wagon wheel.

I'm down on my knees; I blow your horn.
We painted hunters, let's hide & go seek.
I'm from under your spell; I wish you well.

My clothes all in shreds, we had our turn.
My eyes are wide open. I made a mistake.
Rock me, baby; roll me like a wagon wheel.

I won't worry good times; seeds been sown.
Patted down and sprouting, I'm wide awake.
I'm from under your spell; I wish you well.

Yes, rock me; roll me like a wagon wheel.

Home Is Where Relief Is

I was on the roof of the storehouse when my mother
left to return to Baltimore with her better son. Forest
air was cool & thin, the sun bright above puffy white

clouds drifting, shaping moments of shade. Memories.
I am rooted up, torn by a childhood past. Abandoned.
Like an attached shed, I was her father's creation. Rot

was hidden in the supporting wall. I pried boards with
a crowbar, sweated, banged, loosened, exposed rafters.
I tore the roof down to a ragged skeleton, four two by

fours, I sat on the edge, feet on the ladder, northward
over watermelon vines spreading. Country life is rich
soil and green silence. My mother is gone back again

to a red-brick row house in Yale Heights, a small yard
in back with alley & a front porch & yard with flowers.
Generating life is a body's gift, but not nearly enough.

Cousin Susie Moore Is Dead

Before sunset, tree frog's ringing chorus
forced mockingbird into silence. He calls
for rain, Mama used to say, when she had
all her folk memory. Her focused mind is
elsewhere as Malvina's grandchildren pass
away. Monday morning two were left; now
she is the last. Oh, it's tough to grow old
knowing death cannot be escaped. No one
to rescue you from a certainty. There she
lies on her bed, alone, head in hand, milky
blue eyes, waiting on him in dread with
faith & hope the sun'll rise one more day,
to breakfast one more family morning, one
breath more to dream, before lights go out.

Meditation on Insects

I sip more coffee to pry eyes wide & be free, a blue
jay. On two hours sleep I drive, haul, lift boards &
roofing to build shed for stove wood. Winter winds

will suck tears, turn us all to ruin if we be not ants in
their moving dirt & storing up because of a cell they
lack, no question mark in their brain. I am more than

cog in a network of impulses. I recall my childhood.
I have my regrets what I might have done for family
if I had said Yes when I said No. Ants live tiny lives

so how Tinka & me came to be is a No mystery. We
beyond reasoning. My life as my day ends in a sweat
hot enough for an air conditioner. My brow in mouth

of skeletal shed ponders swooping air zig-zags: long-
tailed mosquito hawk snapping prey as a child scoops
up candy from a tray. Full moon rises blood red over

graveyard. No omen but lack of time for mockingbird,
his black crow blues. Sunsets are made to take note of
pain. Beyond us, we more than skull house for insects.

Get Up Dead Man: Blues Villanelle #2

Get up dead man, help me carry my load.
Tinka, I was 21 when you went away.
I can't make my boss man feel satisfied.

A doctor cut you up & stretched you out.
Years I cried tears before that awful day.
Get up dead man, help me carry my load.

At 65, you became a myth—devout.
At 16, your hair had turned wisdom gray.
I can't make my boss man feel satisfied.

You caught on quick what life is all about.
Dad, I asked why; you knew what to say.
Get up dead man, help me carry my load.

There are days we stumble & go without.
You worked moons; I learned how to pray.
Our boss man never wants to be satisfied.

Let they who must, go to church & shout.
Spirit Man, rise up beyond what they play.
Get up dead man, help me carry my load.

My boss man he's not feeling satisfied.

Trinidad Lady at Club Paradise

This forest morning at Jerusalem, sun shines down hot as an island girl's smile. In shadows she dances at Club Paradise, whining zebra pants thigh split in air heavy as a wet blouse on bare nipples. Today, I daydream what loving could have been me standing on the side of a roof with hammer, nails, & boards. At the bar with our drinks—my scotch on rocks, her rum & coke—we talked about spoors & shades: she as a soldier in Iraq, me a writer against warmongers,

she about her divorce of a Virginia man & me of her startling beauty as mom of a grown son; she of night work at a post office; me how her eyes sparkled; she of never again binding herself to a man; & me about an old man living in a digital world on a mountain in a timeless world of ideas so vague only overeducated boys with heads filled with regurgitated philosophies might drink pale femininity in dark drums. Climbing through clouds I kissed her a good night sweet Irene.

Dreading Distrust & Reparations

My fate comes in focus, dead pine holding up time,
a no man's land, by live tree limbs. The sky cracks.
I slam down. Falling covers up what was. One step

more I sink in what might be. I portend a work that
is more tedium, a new lover. I recreate for memory
far more in blue midnight. I'm fixing a carpenter's

storehouse roof falling in decades. The builder who
sired me passed: I barely a man. His grandchildren
left as they wandered crook to hollow—furniture,

records, tools, books, mildew, mold, dirt. All in ruin.
Rodents, ants, rain gnaw holes with no care of legacy
sought. The floor & walls fall like roof. There's cost

for resurrecting roofs & walls. I scratch my left palm.
Air, wood, stone take up the tasks of dying ancestors.
Goodbye mystery keepers! Corporate media cover-

up bombs falling in Lebanon! Our war economy rocks
us gently into a nod. Butterflies still dance silent songs.
Drums fade as a moon repairs toward tall dark treetops.

Reparations along the Nottoway

In this dark, damp forest, tree frogs & insects sound
the night in the bend of Nottoway, river of *Nadowa*,
native god. His sacred blood was spilled so long ago
by invaders. Arrowheads were dug up at Stony Creek
where his *Cheroenhaka* mothers used to camp.

Now, fawn bound through fields of soybeans hearing
the roar of engines. Few hands are used these days to
till soil when machines are quicker than black fingers
& stiffer than black backs. The Snakes, forest hunters,
warred against both markets & Christ. . . Tarred roads

didn't exist when I was a boy. When Mama was twelve,
there were no dirt roads, but wagon trails & horse paths
on which she rode Duke bareback to the doctor's office
up in Jarratt Town. Her father owned 75 acres of forest
then. The grandchildren of slaves left fields for big city

dreams centuries after the Snake people lost the skies to
their conquerors. Scattered over seven states & Canada,
they gather to reclaim bloodlines—ridgepoles stored in
ledgers & museums. Can we be made whole with bones,
ancient spirits wandering among cypress, oaks & pines?

Reparations as an Artful Enterprise

I've nailed down almost all the boards on the storehouse roof—
an enterprise started as one of collaboration & cooperation like
all beginnings on the shores of discovery. In body, soul, or spirit
there's always an injury, excuse, or treaty violation when people
go their own ways in reaching a cave. But even there interlopers
find a way to your door seeking favor or betrayal. Dream drivers
assault the brain with verbs, dress you in demoralizing adjectives

to conjugate bad blood. Some tasks like carpentry compel more
measuring than dropping seeds in tilled soil, holding handles
of a plow, riding machines. More delicacy is needed repairing or
restoring. Body construction requires a vision of worth. Richness
of soil or temper or weather is of little matter. I'm for a building
lasting beyond one's self, or one's bellyache. Now I go it alone.

Divine Reparations Are Eternal

August revival nears. Bombs fall & boost the market in
winding sheets for Gaza babies. Palestine is crumbling.

Here at Jerusalem, a golden sun squints in tall pines; soft
breezes are a woman's hand on cheeks. Brown eyes look

up to a blue, melting iceberg mind. Our garden bellows
out a bounty of snaps, tomatoes, spinach, kale, cabbages,

lima beans. White bell flowers with red centers bloom on
the lawn as birds perch in silence, a sultry stillness, dry &

scorching. Gaza night skies without moon & stars roar. It is
no Good Humor truck. Here cool insects orbit pole light,

bats night-time feast. Tree frogs cry rain in rustling leaves.
It's no paradise. Mosquitoes & gnats fly sorties in my ear.

To Hell with Blackness & Nationalism

I sit on the screened porch, not painfully hot, across
from cemetery, & listen for God's voice to speak as

my ancestor. On days (nights) he visits me, if dead
I'd ask, "What did you say?" I lament my deafness.

In a world filled with horrors, kidnapping & insects,
clanging sickness, terror & death I find it difficult to

measure what is Truth. Daily, I perform celibate tasks.
Today, I shelled butter beans a few hours. A next day,

I return to roofing my father's storehouse. Doubtful, I
scour half-belief pages, a scholarly book on intestinal

blackness. Croaking, I raise questions. Who speaks to
me across time & space? Two car beams bore a damp

dark swamp silence, a winding otherworld forest road.
What! God or Satan, I ask? I hammer nail in tar paper.

IV

August Revival

Resurrection

My forest refuge is in half-moon heat—a sawdust leisure.
Our harvest out-sizes every kitchen table. We shelled lima
beans today for the winter & we quilt dialogue of religious
values in Langston's Aunt Hagar, her lapses & forgiveness.
She fancied stewed tomatoes for revelry. Weltering leaves
turn brown like flesh under summer sun: a rich crop, huge
fruit in stages of ripeness, hanging: reds, yellows, & green.
Black life is filled with solemnity: Jimboy grounded out in a
car accident in Germany. Yet golden rain trees live on in his
son Sandy. *Not Without Laughter* shags sky-blue nights.

August Revival

The sadness ends only to begin again. It is our legacy
at Jerusalem. The best/worst began/ended Monticello
in Sally Hemings. The worst/best began/ended again
in Nathaniel Turner, rape of mother and his lynching
at Jerusalem on Nottoway. Our ancestors christened

in freedom our community remembrance of his deeds,
sacrifice & slaughter of Satan in man. All was forgot in
my mother's generation the story of the revival of God
in man. 2nd Sunday services—nightly writhing to Friday
testifying & preaching—pointless vigils. Memory fails

in half literate & humble that worked fields & sawmills.
Defeat after victory. On clear summer nights moons are
yellow, a setting sun bright orange glow, race harbinger
of the same: eloquence of dead poets & prophets always
getting it wrong. Congregants—walkers & wheelchairs

the next world pressing upon them, had their deliverance
from cotton & tobacco fields. Absent are over-burdened
youth, by low wages, frisked, & prison guards cooked as
crab-claws, fires unquenched in this holy place, a tedious
suffering army of outcasts, a sky of milk-toast resolutions.

My Woman Is This Forest

God sends Sunday in many colors. Moon
waxes full in purple sky, shining sane
sight on us. A walnut skinned woman smiles
mulberry trees. It's apple ripe weather.
Beside red bricked porch, a mockingbird sings.
This pine top forest my African mom,
harsh yellow inscrutable moods, soothing
labor of vermillion arms. Look! Here is
a blues lover with pumpkin sunshine in
her mouth. A toad frog tongues insect flight.
A deep-rooted childhood walks well-known paths
to fishing pond in Sansi Swamp, where slave
runaways escape bloodhound yapping heels.
Magnolia blossoms turn brown in black hands.

Romance Has No Natural Death

Old lovers are unlike garden plants that
are cut down & plowed under, the fruit
stored away in freezer bags & canning
jars to be eaten on cold tomorrows.
Their skin & bone stripes are mouthed in prayer
letters secreting daggers & goober dust.
One deletes. Still they rise up in wet dreams
prowling redemption routes; in one's nightmares
snarling behind dark veils, monochrome by
sunken ground, voiceless, still befuddled, on
how legends fall down & worm off the page
in cures for a blameless itch. Tearing, they
walk away, tossing dirt on coffin lid.
Store rooms can lift spirits in darkest hours.

Women Who Care for the Weak

Early morning I finished tar papering a woodshed roof.
Solitude & revelry leave me for fugitive heroes/victims

like my cat Bobo & Jimmy Baldwin. Each bares scars
of blackness in America. My cat lounges tooth & claw.

The Exile praises his unwed mother. Our kitchen table
forums my aunt laughing misery in its face. She draws

back from husks of ancestors. Her father's sweat bricks
an old house. He called his daughter when illness fell in

'69 like stars to earth. A grandma groans her faith fixing
meals for her 95-year-old mother. I drove home pass a

dark woman pushing a baby carriage—passing cars light
her way. Full moon casts purple shadows, flickering film.

Our lives at Jerusalem rebound as graveyards grow close.
In smoke panoramas, these women live us & we in them.

Chickens Coming Home

Mothers unlike war corpses forgive failure.
We canned ten jars of black-eyed peas, today.
We winter wage chasms, earthquakes, storm & floods.
Rabbit & plucked wild turkey on menu to
stomach grunts of gluttony on Wall Street.
Apple contracts flew the coop to Asia.
Factories & wealth pack their boxes & bags.
Koch Bros. & bloodhounds of oil drill, refine
thumb up prices & finger all at gas pump
index to elbow, Italian style. Tongue
between the bones ad men & pundit news.
My cousin now sells pond fish from his truck.
Debt fogged across the river he screams, ducks
Humvees. In the skies, gunships keep firing.

Loving That Other Man

Former-slaves built Jerusalem plank by
hewed plank, paced off acres, climbed up to white
steeple, where misery loses its grip.
Fog thickens after a day of showers.
Mama's 95th, full moon rises high.
Nat Turner too wondered whether we'd learn
before the Day of Reckoning comes near
during August Revival. Like Baldwin
he turned to Holy Ghost meditations
against dangerous powers—rape, incest
lynching, posted heads & genocide—all
for the gods of profit, our ancestors
their murderous nightmare. Eyeless bones on
the Atlantic floor won't tell the whole truth.

Don't Say Goodbye to Truth

Mockingbird trilled a quick tune from a limb
then flew off. No dew glistens on this lawn.
Apologists for Monticello fade
as Uncle Jeff's lived life becomes neon.
Southern winds stir the weeping willow near
the reddening apple tree. Under calm
mountain skies, he traded families for wine
& French spirits. A hawk's fortune is bleak
in this shadowless morning. Driven by
ghostly monsters we herald luxury
as a shallow privilege of skin politics
divined by racial reasoning that changes
for oil profits, Middle East regime change.
Tree frogs croak more bloody bombs yet to fall.

Good Night Sweet Irene

Mockingbird's packed up for warmer climes.
He's making the rounds saying his goodbyes.
His courtships and taunting of strolling crows
sink into spring memory where he comes
with the tilling of soil. Autumn coolness
exudes watermelon ripeness. White bell
flowers fall from the lawn bush. Mason jar
tops sealed tight for winter are yesteryear
tasks of ancients of a golden sunset.
Revival prayers at Jerusalem
butt the roof like thunder claps with flashes,
lighting up the cemetery tree line.
A windless downpour drenches the tin roof.
Me, I'm sinking in a Mockingbird song.

Last Call Dreaming

The damp forest is domed in dark purple as
stars twinkle crisp and clear. The moon rises
after midnight. My head says no to pillow.
On New Orleans internet radio
station old blues records keep on spinning.
The river and lake keep rising, bursting
through levees; our people are still screaming,
still wading, waving from rooftops, to be
rescued. Water, water everywhere, none
to quench thirst; food, food is everywhere but
there is none for black stomachs; babies cry,
no ears can hear, some hearts get harder. Here
in this forest on dry land, it's no dream.
Bluesmen still squeeze out life in Big Easy.

Dispelling the Darkness

Terror bombings in Iraq & Lebanon
make us cry. Hills & hills of skulls. Our
histories filled with bloody revenge. We
sight X in computerized guns & roll out
tanks. Hands cheer the counted dead.
Bulbs flash blindly our identities &
manhood. We suck our knives, hold

our shackled tongues. Drones & freedom
birds roar/zip by overhead as anti-aircraft
guns fire. Fatigues bulge in crotch armor,
topped with riddled helmets. Blood sinks
shifting sand. My brain calls up nightmare
gunfights, drug raiders at my door mauling
black boys with legs spread. Children lost.
I wrestle fishes of sacrifice that get each

of us through. Gum trees of swamp forests
wag like dog heads swinging near ground,
wretchedly for three centuries. My soul
packs up bloody garments we wear for the
end of a final journey. Gods slam-dunk our
bronze skulls—families suffer devastation
dreamscapes as beasts truck on metal legs.

Defying Raging Night

Darkness stretches out in this new moon forest like
highway pitch. Still I hear mockingbird in walked
worn wooded paths through tangling bushes. On
such nights, I hurried home on snaking dirt roads,
in ancient cypress swamps, entangled limbs of oaks
overarch dirt roads, as stars twinkle in a purple sky.
When I was a boy ringing insect sounds affirmed

my faith. I've walked too red hills of Bukavu
and knelt by the glassy waters of Lake Kivu,
spoke with the god of rivers, crying out ties as
solemn as oaths on holy books. At the Grand
Marché, I saw a man his torso on a board roll
himself along with padded hands. On the plain
of Goma I lighted from a prop plane to relieve

myself. It was where tribal men, women, and
children sought refuge from rage and machete
seeking blood-lust, I was Kongo, then, survivor
of that nightmare passage with strange tongues,
the spirit-killing crammed sadness of iron chains.
I've known black wonders soothing enough to
write letters in hope of a Mockingbird spring.

Up on Pisgah

Poets, artists (all sorts) travel by digital satellite.
They soar above wooded horizons to reach us in
low ground. They draw me up to heady high places
so we see a world yet to come. Beyond walls, we
seek more than implements of removal. My eyes
mouthpiece the dead, rather than trade. I conjure

Jerusalem's men of vision & sweat, scheming in
blue smoke. I liberate my worth from despots &
doorsills—my body tangled in barbed wire. I'm
brisk breezes in the lawn's bell flowers—a sage.
Pines, oaks across the cemetery possess a crystal
clarity, rocking under wind gusts their limbs this

cool August day. I'm a poet searching for a home
on a Tanzanian beach as clocks spin backward to
traditions with no gods of anarchy & disbelief. I
reside in a yet-to-cease time, where soul catchers
—whose power & arms float kennels east to west,
factory to fields—die from a thousand paper cuts.

Sonnet for 22 August 1831

If we slipped away unknown into dark
forests often as black men did so long
ago in secret coves like Booze Island
in the Loco woods & converse in tongues
dine on dripping hot roast pig, smoking yams
with moonshine & brandy, we could win all.
Nobody will know what we put down or
the cross we pick up. A faith communion
will fuel acts heroic—sacrificial.
Beyond our master's grasp & driver's whip,
free of fears & reckonings, gifted flights
across the dark purple skies will birth a
bold love & a daring defiance. For
seven determined men can rock the world.

Sonnet for Ancestors

It's the comic, buck-and-wing, your field-working
hips that charm white remembrance—waking screams.
Over a barrel centuries, red back
stripes were your badge of courage. Moon rises,
waxes & wanes. Archaic lines live yet.
CIA-MI-5/think tanks study
the tactics & terror of runaways.
We bluesmen mask as birds with green goggles,
disarm Satan's swarm with a song cocktail
of shame, guilt, tears, blood. Where the gangsters at
to smash marble monument heroes, bronze
words of regime change behind dark sun shades?
We waking up to what granny wants to hear.
In free space, we defy the hell we live.

Blind Woman with Guitar

On a dark stage she's in a blue spotlight.
Her walnut skin/shell displays her passion.
She ripples nerves, vibrates the smoky room
as her fingers pluck chords, black-water notes.
She's Southern blind boys with eyes, a corkscrew.
Her critics are a lost generation.
She strums and sings of museums in her
head, of masterworks leaning sideways in
her breath space on unearthed walls. She escapes
the con-man fictions of social scientists.
Her voice goes silent as she picks her way
through the cotton fields of her memory.
Her song rises on swing low chariot,
thumb blackening Camelia knight terror.

Sonnet for Reality Men

Whether in New Orleans or Harlem, they mask
as good shepherds or real-deal men. Uptown
or downtown they are fairy lights. Call them
Momus, Comus, or Protesus— ghettologists,
guards of those sweet belly brownstones and
public houses we call home. They hail us as
foreigners prone to vice. None patronize
writers and poets who diet on Marx, Freud,
and Reich—experts of chaos. Through little
plastique doors glued to chest these clowns
drumbeat it's fun to be Negro. Warehousing
guns & drugs, big bellies spread. Criminal big
bucks build high-rise condos. Shameless they
shackle & cage us like beasts.

War Is Not a Time of Joy

On a crescent moon night, my brain's noisy
as a factory floor. No bombs fall here.
No troops on these forest roads. No gunships
with spotlights to block the purple carpet
of stars There's silence of insects, a dog's.
barking. My nightmares come from a knowing—
a deep-seated cumbrous fear we don't care
enough. I'm trapped but not fooled. This captive
has no joyful jig for my cruel captors.
My Manifesto's inscribed with plain script
cursing warmongers & moneylenders.
Complications ain't love around the house.
My chocolate don't make me feel so sweet.

Sonnet for Albert Murray

In the cemetery pine mockingbird
pipes a few notes that make a difference.
In my head it's a child's voice that speaks of
love, death, the spoils of war. I press my lips
to sound them out again, finger the holes
& blow. He's silent. A carnation sound
stirs green leaves of a nearby oak. Passions,
a hip/cool Duke Ellington elegance
wag my cat ears. A black snake startles me
from my reverie. A dark scene holds grief
at arm's length. Grandma's hope burns out for me:
a poet is more than an undertaker,
even if you end up with nothing. When you
study a blues ballad the whole world shuffles.

Blues Sonnet for an Empty Bed

It's four in the morning. . . I'm rolling &
tumbling. Street lights on my window pane. Ma
Rainey sings blues on the radio. She's
had nothing but trouble from con men who
crowd her game. Woman to woman she dusts
her nose with cocaine for midnight divas.
Woman of fashion, she's on stage wide-eyed.
Hanging on the rafters I wanted her
to feel me. How blind she is to my scars
She asks me how I feel. I appreciate
the hoodoo of her concerns, the smell of
her roots, twigs, leaves & flora. Still I walk
the floor nights to forget how her touching
words keep reaching out for loaded dice.

Women with Men in Prison

—for Pedro

He's not in Abu Ghraib a black bag
over his head, his genitals exposed
on film by a mocking female GI.
He's not at Guantanamo enchained by
CIA/Pentagon memos, tortured
by water, bright lights around the clock. No,
he's down on Southampton County Farm
on a work detail in Boykins paying
thirty dollars a week for room & board.
His wits play bid whist with his woman two
hours on Sunday, throughout his slave-long day.
If he gets the blues thinking she not alone,
he sings, I didn't get 25 to life.
In six months she'll be a card-player's wife.

Mining Black Males

Tonight a four year old child
is dead. He was here
in the house this afternoon.
A stepfather, my cousin, sits
on a cot in Southampton jail,
his head buried in thoughtless hands
wondering how fragile life changes (ends)
suddenly, unexpectedly. A mother mindless.
A grandmother prays continually.
A child is dead tonight.
Heaven's flashlight clicks on & off
across the purple night skies for hours.
It's too tragic for tears.

Under a Dark Cloud

—for Marquis

Storms swoop in like hawks, as they sometimes do in Jerusalem. Talons grip us. Trees fall across pathways, power lines fail us, roofs fly off in high winds. That's how we were late August when dark clouds settled on forest pine tops straining up to the heavens. A pithless, tugging headline savages flesh, "Local Man Murders Wife's Four-Year-Old Mixed Race Son." For two days, a green mile, family rain-soaked: Child beaten dies in restraint. Swamps rise & spill in low ground. We prey for the strong—grandma walks midnight—souls wail.

We'll never start hearts loving if we flood out life divine. Hatred. A mother, father, and child balloon. Truths don't flow out mirrors. At courthouse handcuffed, he sweats & steps before the bar. His muscles bulge. Tears trail down his spine, knees buckle. His artlessness no help in granite detachment. Suspicions engulf evidence: cops set traps of threats & plea bargains. Skies clear blue. Winds & rumor die down. The state cleans up blood & ruin. No love here. Steel bars bang shut. A court fashions man a slave for life.

Sonnet for Carter

A hawk soars, wheels over Jerusalem
and flies off in Christ crossed skies, familiar
visions. Showers fall from dark gray clouded
eyes—R.I.P. tragic funerals.
Last night our prayers for a four-year-old,
an absent black father and a wayward
white mother who had only now begun
to root and bloom in uncultivated
red soil. He lies on a loveless love seat,
pale, his pink lips swollen—one hand in jeans,
a cap, his toys, a poster of photos
of his false childhood, mangled. We fall down
with loss we carry into tear-soaked pews
while crows and ants feast on flesh left behind.

Sonnet for Bailing Out

Dark clouds drift toward the coast, unveil a full
moon that cast graveyard shadows. Thunder
booms in the distance no tales of love's embrace.
More flooding I think before week's end.
Tree frogs keep crying damp & cool autumn air.
Omens blend with blood stories on treetop
horizons. Green sparrows flee mockingbird-
crow conflicts. Blind justice deep-ends balance

on spider web scales. A grieving mother
grows sad stories in jail cell—minds snared
in no horn blowing on signs. All night long
she cries goodbyes to son's dust around her
neck. Clearing away a farce, he rises an
innocent in the state's big payback.

Ode to Walls

1. You rose from the stony earth with bloodstained groans
to bestow birth and growth to civilization.
You were created first to support roofs
and ceilings against the sun and storm—
mud huts and the wooden longhouse
to divide space for privacy
a barrier to moving earth, stone, and water.

You've outgrown your modest grace for mural beauty
& art. You're upright now for prisons and trophies.

O, Ancient One, monstrous stone Serpent that will
not fall. You snake your way speaking volumes
from the Great Wall of China to Israel's West Bank
barrier to northern Mexican boundaries to secure
residences here in America. Your strength mortared
dead men's bones to ideology.

2. You metamorphosed Deceiver, descendent of Satan,
tossed from Heaven, so long ago. You Separator of
Togetherness! We breathe your essence deeply
the skull's wolf bane. Our soul's categories embrace
nothingness not flowing, not permeable to warmth and
care, no connecting doors to enter rooms of ethical
ruminations. As mechanical as industrial centuries we
return to a hotel hallway, change our masks, our business
suits before entering another orange toga fantasy of
ourselves. Our precarious lives demand we call such
deceit—poise, freedom from terror.

www.ingramcontent.com/pod-product-compliance
Lightning Source LLC
Chambersburg PA
CBHW031203090426
42736CB00009B/771